THE
BOOK FOR HOT
FOOD FREAKS
HOT
WHO ARE JUST CRAZY
ABOUT CHILI

Angus&Robertson
An imprint of HarperCollins*Publishers*

Mussels with Chili, Garlic and Basil 32 ★ Steak Fajitas 33 ★
Madras Prawn Curry 35 ★ Pork Salad with Chili, Peanuts
and Ginger 36 ★ Tandoori Chicken 39 ★ Chili Con Carne 40 ★
Spicy Chicken. Livers 42 ★
Prawns in Garlic and Chili Sauce 44 ★
Thai Barbecued Chicken 46 ★ Seafood in Green Chili Sauce 47 ★
Salmon with Coconut Coriander Salsa 50 ★
Chili Pepper Yabbies 51 ★

ENTS

ZING! 52 ★

SALSAS, SAMBALS AND PICKLES

Red Chili Salsa 52 ★ Hot Peach Pickle 53 ★
Eggplant Pickle 54 ★ Pickled Chilies 55 ★
Hot Pickled Vegetables 56 ★ Bengal Apple Chutney 58 ★
Stuffed Chilies 59 ★ Egg Sambal 61 ★
Mixed Vegetable Sambal 62 ★
Potato Sambal 63 ★

HOT FOOD is synonymous with herbs, spices, and, of course, chilies. In these recipes many different kinds of herbs and spices are used, some more often than others, but the one thing all these *recipes* have in common is **HEAT!** The different types of herbs and spices are all used not just to add fire to the food, but flavor, color and aroma also.

Hot food simply wouldn't be as hot without **CHILIES**.

INTR✸D

There are dozens of varieties, from fiery, hot ones to those that are sweet and mild. If you live near a specialist food supplier you can experiment with real **MEXICAN**, Thai and Indian chilies, usually available dried in packets, canned, or bottled. However, you can make do with any fresh and dried chilies, or even substitute a mixture of capsicums (peppers) and dried chili powder.

Fresh chilies come in red, green, yellow and black,

and in various sizes. Usually the smaller they are, the **hotter** they taste. *Dried chilies* are widely available and, if necessary, can be soaked in hot water for a few minutes before using. You can make your own dried chilies by threading together different varieties and hanging them near a sunny spot until they are well dried. Then store them in an airtight container. Ground chilies, chili paste or dried chili flakes can be substituted in most dishes if fresh chilies are not available.

The main VARIETIES of herbs used in these recipes are basil, bay leaves, coriander, marjoram, mint, oregano, and thyme. The main spices used are CHILI **POWDER**, cinnamon, cloves, cumin, curry powder, fenugreek seeds, garam masala, ginger, mustard, paprika, pepper, poppy seeds and turmeric. All are readily available in dried form if you cannot find a fresh supply from your local store or **MARKET.**

AND KEEP YOUR HANDS AWAY FROM YOUR FACE AND EYES, AND FROM THOSE OF CHILDREN. THE OILS THE CHILI SKINS EXUDE ARE VOLATILE.

A CHILI

Poblano

A reasonably mild dark green chili, about 10 cm to 12 cm (4 to 5 in) long and used for *Stuffed Chilies* (see page 59). When dried the poblano is called an *ancho*, and sometimes (incorrectly) *pasilla* pods. When you cannot get poblanos, substitute banana chilies with the insides rubbed with chili powder.

Jalapeño

This is the most commonly canned and pickled chili. It is about 6 cm (2½ in) long, and is fat and juicy. When fresh they can be green, yellow, or reddish. When dried and smoked they are called *chipotles*, and are widely available in cans. As a substitute for fresh jalapeño, use any fresh hot chili. Pickled jalapeño chilies can be eaten separately as a snack.

Serrano

A small, thin, hot, red or green chili, widely available throughout the world, the serrano chili is perhaps the easiest to grow at home. The flavor is strong and rich. Red birdseye chilies can be substituted.

GUIDE

7

Black CHILIES

Also called *chilaca* or *chile negro* these chilies are long, dark and hot.
When they are dried, they are sometimes called ***chile pasilla***.
If you cannot find them, substitute any dark colored, medium, hot
fresh CHILI, or capsicum (pepper) and extra chili powder, if desired.

Habanero Chilies

These pretty, lantern-shaped **CHILIES** in varying shades of red
and green are among the hottest chili varieties in the world.
From the West Indies, they are deathly HOT.

Yellow OR Green Chilies

Any pale yellow or green chili is usually called *guero* or 'blond'.
Small yellow 'wax chilies', usually available bottled, are also
known as *guero*. They are generally fairly hot, and are used fresh
or pickled but not dried. Do not confuse them with the THAI
yellow chili known as *prik yuak* which is a pale yellowish-green
and is very mild, being usually stuffed and served as a snack.

California OR Anaheim

Usually mild to medium hot, fresh, long red chilies. These chilies
are suitable for stuffing if you can find any large enough.

They are similar in appearance, taste and intensity to the chilies grown in Kashmir known as *kashmiri* **or** *degi mirich*. They can be used fresh when a red color is required in a dish, but are often used in dried form.

Cayenne Chilies

These are about 3 in (8 cm) long and used fresh or dried for their hot flavor as well as to add a red color to a dish. They are often ground for use in cooking and as a condiment. Also known as *prik chee far* in THAI cookery.

Kashmiri Chilies

These are long, and a deep red color, similar to California chilies. Mild in flavor they are used for their color. Also known as *degi mirich* and *kashmiri mirich* in Indian cookery.

Thai 'Bird's Eye' CHILIES

Also known as *prik khee noo suan*, these are the ones which give Thai food its reputation for hot tastes. They are tiny red or green chilies no more than 1.25 cm (½ in) in length and intensely HOT. They may have been so named for their eye-like shape, or because mynah birds love to eat them and usually become very talkative afterwards.

This pointed, rich red chili is used in hot Indonesian dishes.

Banana CHILI

This is a pale green sweet fresh chili, about 14 to 16 cm (5½ to 6 in) long, which ripens to a pale pinky orange. Though it really has a flavor more like a CAPSICUM (pepper) it is useful for stuffing. Rub the insides with chili powder to give the banana chili a bite.

CHILI PaSTE

Also known as *nam prik pao* and sometimes called Chili Paste in Bean Oil, Burnt Mild or Roasted Chili Paste, this is an ingredient in many Thai recipes, including the famous Tom Yam soups. The paste is made in Thailand and sold in squat jars in the condiments or Thai sections of Asian foodstores. It is made from dried chilies, dried shrimp, roasted onion, garlic, sugar and tamarind juice. A small amount of fresh or dried chili can be used as a substitute.

CHILI SAUCE

There are countless recipes for chili sauces, to bottle as condiments and to make fresh to accompany noodles and rice,

Sauce for Chicken' (it goes with everything, in fact). There are many recipes for home-made traditional spicy hot sauces — no traditional Asian meal would be complete without at least one.

CHILI FLAKES

These are crushed, dried chilies, usually with their seeds, that are used in many recipes in preference to whole chilies or chili powder, the latter tending to give a sauce a slightly gritty feel.

DRIED CHILIES

Dried CHILIES are even richer in vitamin C than fresh ones and can add special richness and depth to a sauce. As a rule, you usually need to lightly roast or dry-fry the chilies to bring out their flavor, and then soak them in warm water until they soften. Do not soak them too long or you will leave their flavor behind in the water. Do not try to remove their skin, and either slice or purée them with or without their seeds and veins, depending on how much heat you require. Remember the heat in chilies is in their veins, or membranes, not their seeds.

If you cannot find the chili specified in a recipe, use your own mixture of locally **DRIED CHILIES**, capsicum (pepper), chili powder or paprika, or substitute one type of dried chili for another. Below is a list of the most common dried chilies with a brief description of their appearance and flavor.

ANCHO○

The most commonly used dried chili, the ancho chili is the pablano ripened to a deep red, and dried. It should still be flexible when dried with a deep reddish brown wrinkled skin. The ancho is easily confused with a mulato which should be more reddish black and not as sharp and fruity as the ancho. Both are large and squat, about 10 cm (4 in) long by about 8 cm (3 in) wide. *Chile ancho* has a sharp flavor but is not a particularly hot chili. Sometimes ancho chilies are incorrectly labelled as **PASILLA** pods, but the squat shape suggests it is an ancho, not a pasilla.

GUAJILLO○

After the ancho, the guajillo is the most commonly used dried chili. It is smooth with a tough skin of a deep maroon, thin and about 12 cm (5 in) long. It is medium hot to hot, with a sharp flavor. You may have to discard the skin to purée.

PASILLA OR DRIED NEGRO

This is the dried version of the fresh chili negro (black chili) or *chilaca*, and is black, shiny and wrinkled. It is long and thin, about 15 cm (6 in) long and 3 cm (1 in) wide. Pasilla ranges in flavor from mild to hot and has a rich flavor. Sometimes you will find ancho chilies labelled as *pasilla* pods, but true *chile pasilla* or negro, are long and thin, not squat shaped chilies like the ancho.

MULATO

Similar in size and appearance to an ancho chili, but with a sweeter, more chocolaty taste than the fruitier, sharper flavored ancho. The mulato is mild to moderately hot and dark reddish-black.

CHIPOTLE

This is the jalapeño chili, ripened, dried and smoked. Widely available in jars or cans, they are very hot and are always used with seeds and veins intact.

Pumpkin and Coconut Cream Soup

(Gaeng Liang Fak Tong) T H A I L A N D

400 g (13 oz) pumpkin, peeled and cut in 2 cm (¾ in) cubes
1 tablespoon lemon or lime juice
100 g (3½ oz) green (uncooked) prawns or dried shrimp
2 medium-sized onions
¼ teaspoon shrimp paste
2 fresh chilies, seeded or 2 teaspoons roasted chili paste (optional)
1 tablespoon finely chopped lemon grass
300 ml (10 fl oz) water
3 cups (750 ml/24 fl oz) coconut milk (reserve thick cream from top)
1 tablespoon fish sauce
1 teaspoon sugar
½ teaspoon pepper
80 g (2½ oz) fresh basil leaves, reserving some for garnish

1 Sprinkle pumpkin with lemon juice and let it stand for about 20 minutes. Shell and devein fresh prawns or wash dried shrimp.

2 In a food processor, combine prawns, onions, shrimp paste, chilies, lemon grass and a little water, and blend to a smooth paste.

3 Combine 300 ml (10 fl oz) water with thin coconut milk in a large saucepan and stir in the paste, fish sauce, sugar and pepper. Bring to the boil, then reduce heat, stirring with a wooden spoon to ensure smooth consistency. Add pumpkin, simmer gently for about 20 minutes until pumpkin is tender. Taste to see if any seasoning is required.

4 Just before serving, stir in basil and reserved thick coconut cream, garnish with a sprinkle of extra basil leaves.

SERVES 4

Mulligatawny Soup
INDIA

2 tablespoons ghee
1 onion, thinly sliced
1 tablespoon cracked black pepper
½ teaspoon ground ginger
2 teaspoons ground turmeric
1 tablespoon ground coriander
1 teaspoon chili powder
1 kg (2 lb) chicken pieces
4 cups (1 litre/35 fl oz) water

1 Melt ghee in a saucepan and sauté onion until tender. Add pepper, ginger, turmeric, coriander and chili.

2 Add chicken pieces and water. Bring to the boil, reduce heat to low, cover, simmer for 45 minutes or until chicken is tender.

SERVES 4 TO 6

15

Spicy Skewered Meatballs
AUSTRALIA

500 g (1 lb) minced beef
1 onion, finely chopped
1 egg, lightly beaten
1 cup (60 g/2 oz) fresh breadcrumbs
2 tablespoons tomato sauce
2 tablespoons sweet chili sauce
1 teaspoon ground cumin
1 tablespoon chopped fresh parsley

1 Place beef, onion, egg, breadcrumbs, tomato sauce, chili sauce, cumin and parsley in a bowl and mix well to combine.

2 Roll mixture into small balls. Place 2 meatballs on each skewer and barbeque or grill, turning frequently for 10 minutes or until cooked. Serve with a spicy dipping sauce.

MAKES 18

17

MADAGASCAR A

Pork and Hominy Soup
(Pozole) MEXICO

Pozole is a popular supper dish and is often served at fiestas to celebrate birthdays or weddings, or at Christmas time.

1 kg (2 lb) pork shoulder, cut into large pieces

3 litres (5 pints) water

2 x 500 g (16 oz) cans hominy or corn kernels, drained

2 onions, peeled and finely chopped

1 teaspoon salt

2 cups shredded cabbage, or ½ small cabbage, shredded

8 spring onions, finely chopped

2 carrots, peeled and grated

2 tomatoes peeled, seeded and finely chopped

3 radishes, chopped

3 limes, cut into wedges

3 fresh hot red or green chilies, finely chopped

chili sauce, ready-made or home-made

1 Place pork, water, hominy, onion and salt in a large, heavy based saucepan. Bring to the boil, reduce heat and simmer for 2 to 3 hours, or until the meat is tender.

2 Remove pork from soup and cool. Shred meat. Skim fat from surface of cooled soup. Return shredded meat to soup and reheat.

3 Serve cabbage, spring onions, carrots, tomatoes, radishes, chilies, limes and chili sauce in separate bowls for each person to serve themselves.

SERVES 6

VARIATION: Substitute 2 medium chickens or 1 small turkey for pork. When chicken and turkey are cooked, debone, then add meat to soup.

POZOLE

Hominy is prepared from large white dried corn kernels which you can buy in Mexican markets, but otherwise it is available canned at most good delicatessens. Cooked in a huge soup pot and left to simmer all day long, pozole has many variations, which contain pork, turkey or chicken. In Mexico they use the pig's head for a full-flavored stock. Sometimes ordinary corn is used instead of hominy.

The Devil's Sandwich

(Torta Diablo) M E X I C O

These very hot delights are popular in the markets of Guatalajara, Mexico's second largest city in the state of Jalisco.

50 g (2 oz) butter or margarine
6 large French or Italian bread rolls, split in half
2 cups (500 g/16 oz) shredded cooked beef, chicken or pork
1 small onion, peeled and finely chopped
3 cups (750 ml/24 fl oz) *Red Chili Salsa*, warmed (see page 52)

1 Melt butter or margarine in a pan and cook rolls on each side over a medium heat until golden brown. Remove and set aside to keep warm.
2 Add shredded meat to pan and cook until heated through. Place cooked beef on the bottom half of the rolls, sprinkle with onion and top with roll.
3 Quickly dip whole roll in warmed *Red Chili Salsa* and serve immediately, accompanied by jalapeño chilies and shredded lettuce, if desired.

SERVES 6

Samosas

PASTRY

2 cups (250 g/8 oz) plain flour
½ teaspoon baking powder
1 teaspoon salt
30 g (1 oz) ghee, melted
4 tablespoons plain yoghurt

FILLING

1 onion, finely chopped
2 cloves garlic, crushed
30 g (1 oz) ghee
375 g (12 oz) minced steak
2 teaspoons ground coriander
½ teaspoon ground ginger
½ teaspoon chili powder
1 teaspoon garam masala

1 To Make Pastry: Sift flour, baking powder and salt into a bowl. Add ghee and yoghurt, stir until combined. Knead until dough is smooth.

2 To Make Filling: Melt ghee in a frying pan, sauté onion and garlic until onion is tender.

3 Add mince, coriander, ginger, chili and garam masala. Sauté 10 minutes or until mince is well browned, cool.

4 Fill samosas and deep fry until golden brown. Drain on absorbent paper.

MAKES 15 TO 20

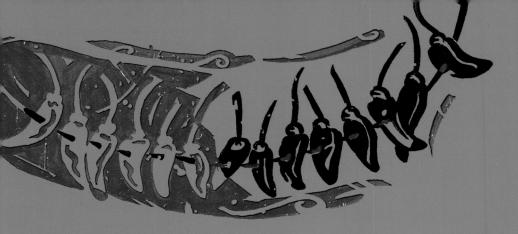

Seasoned Jalapeño Chilies
(Jalapeños con Espices) M E X I C O

3 tablespoons lemon pepper
3 tablespoons coarse salt
1 cup (185 g/6 oz) canned jalapeño chilies, drained
1 small onion, peeled and thinly sliced into rings (optional)

1 Combine lemon pepper and salt. Place in the centre of a
serving plate and arrange chilies and onion rings.

SERVES 4

Savory Toasted Pepitas
(Pepitas Tostada) MEXICO

30 g (1 oz) butter or margarine
1 to 2 cloves garlic, crushed
¼ teaspoon chili powder
250 g (8 oz) pepitas
1 tablespoon Worcestershire sauce

1 Melt butter in a large heavy-based pan and cook garlic and chili powder over a medium heat for 1 minute.

2 Add pepitas and cook, stirring constantly, until they have all popped. Add Worcestershire sauce and mix well to combine. Season to taste with salt if desired.

3 Serve warm or cold.

MAKES 250 G (8 OZ)

23

Spicy Algerian Sardines
GREECE

1 kg (2 lb) fresh sardines
2 tablespoons ground cumin
2 teaspoons chili powder
3 cloves garlic, crushed
2 teaspoons freshly ground black pepper
1½ cups (185 g/6 oz) plain flour
2 eggs, lightly beaten
oil for shallow frying

1 Make a slit on the underside of sardines, gut and remove backbone.

2 Combine cumin, chili, garlic, pepper and flour in a bowl. Dip sardines into egg and then roll in spicy flour. Repeat process with egg and flour, until all the sardines have been coated.

3 Heat oil in a large frying pan. Cook sardines 1 to 2 minutes each side or until brown and tender. Serve as a starter or with salad as a main meal.

SERVES 6 TO 8

FRESH CHILIES ARE A VERY GOOD SOURCE OF VITAMIN C, THE ANTI-INFECTION NUTRIENT.

Barbecued Chili Corn

6 corn cobs with husks
60 g (2 oz) butter, melted
1 teaspoon chili powder
1 teaspoon ground cumin
1 teaspoon ground coriander
1 teaspoon cracked black pepper

1 Remove most of the husks from the corn. Use the remaining husks to wrap around the base of the corn as a handle.

2 Brush corn with combined butter, chili, cumin, coriander and pepper. Barbecue until tender.

SERVES 6

26

Prawn Fritters
INDIA

500 g (16 oz) small cooked prawns, shelled
½ cup (60 g/2 oz) rice flour
½ cup (60 g/2 oz) self-raising flour
1 tablespoon cornflour
1 teaspoon baking powder
¾ cup (90 g/3 oz) semolina flour
½ cup (60 g/2 oz) besan (chickpea flour)
1 large onion, finely chopped
thin slice ginger, finely chopped
½ capsicum (pepper), finely chopped
3 spring onions, chopped
¼ teaspoon ground turmeric
¼ teaspoon ground cumin
¼ teaspoon chili powder
2 eggs, beaten
water as required for mixing
1 cup (250 ml/8 fl oz) oil

1 Combine prawns in a bowl with rice flour, self-raising flour, cornflour, baking powder, semolina flour, besan, onion, ginger, capsicum, spring onions, turmeric, cumin and chili powder.

2 Add beaten eggs and sufficient water to make a thick batter. Allow to stand for 15 minutes.

3 Heat oil in a frying pan over moderate heat. Drop tablespoons of batter, a few at a time, into the oil and fry on both sides until golden brown. Drain on absorbent paper. Serve hot, with tomato sauce or chili sauce as a dip.

MAKES 15 TO 20

Green Sweet Chicken Curry

(Gaeng Keow Wan Gai) T H A I L A N D

2 tablespoons vegetable oil

1½ tablespoons green curry paste, bought or home-made

1 fresh green chili, finely sliced

4 dried Kaffir lime leaves, pre-soaked for 10 minutes, then sliced

3 cups (750 ml/24 fl oz) coconut milk

1 tablespoon fish sauce

2 teaspoons sugar

500 g (16 oz) raw chicken meat, cut into bite-sized pieces

30 g (1 oz) drained canned bamboo shoots, sliced zucchini

or eggplant (aubergine)

30 g (1 oz) fresh or frozen peas

1 tablespoon fresh basil leaves, mint or young citrus leaves

1 In a large saucepan, briefly stir-fry curry paste, chili and lime leaves in oil over a medium heat, then add coconut milk, fish sauce and sugar.

2 When coconut milk begins to bubble, add chicken and, if using, bamboo shoots; turn down heat and simmer to reduce sauce. If it becomes too thick, add a little water or more coconut milk.

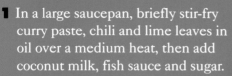

3 When chicken is cooked and sauce is desired consistency, add peas and optional zucchini or eggplant, cooking briefly to retain their firmness.

4 Remove from heat and stir in basil leaves, leaving a few for garnishing.

5 Serve with rice.

SERVES 4

Spicy Barbecued Kebabs
INDIA

Kebabs can be made from minced or cubed meat and are either barbecued or grilled. Essentially dry, they are best served with salads and parathas.

        1 teaspoon poppy seeds
        1 teaspoon ground ginger
        2 teaspoons ground coriander
        1 teaspoon ground turmeric
        ¼ teaspoon chili powder
        1 teaspoon onion juice
        1 tablespoon plain yoghurt
        500 g (16 oz) lamb, beef or pork, cut in 2½ cm (1 in) cubes
        30 g (1 oz) ghee

1 Mix all the spices including the onion juice. Add the yoghurt.

2 Mix the meat well with the yoghurt and spices. Stand at least 30 minutes, preferably overnight.

3 Thread on skewers, cook on a barbecue or under a preheated grill. Turn once and baste occasionally with melted ghee during cooking.

SERVES 4

N THOSE ISLANDS THERE ARE ALSO BUSHES LIKE ROSE BUSHES, WHICH MAKE A FRUIT AS LONG AS CINNAMO

Mussels with Chili, Garlic and Basil

(Pad Hoi Mang Pu) T H A I L A N D

3 fresh chilies, chopped
2 cloves garlic, chopped
1 tablespoon chopped coriander root
3 tablespoons vegetable oil
2 tablespoons oyster sauce
1 tablespoon fish sauce
500 g (1 lb) mussels, scrubbed, beards removed
½ cup (125 ml/4 fl oz) chicken stock or water
4 tablespoons chopped fresh basil or coriander leaves

1 Pound chilies, garlic and coriander root in mortar or process to a rough paste in a food processor. **2** Stir-fry paste with oil in wok or frypan over medium heat until flavors blend well. Add oyster and fish sauces, stir, add mussels and stock. **3** Cover and simmer for 10 minutes until mussels open and are cooked. Taste to see if extra fish sauce or water is needed to balance flavors. Stir in some basil and remove from heat. **4** Arrange mussels on a platter or shallow bowl, pour sauce over them and serve with rice or a salad.

SERVES 4

Steak Fajitas
(Fajitas de Carne) M E X I C O

1 kg (2 lb) lean skirt or round
steak
1 tablespoon olive oil
small bunch fresh coriander,
chopped
12 tortillas, warmed

SIDE DISHES

peeled and sliced Spanish onion
grated cheese
chopped radishes
chopped tomato
shredded lettuce
diced cucumber
yoghurt or sour cream
guacamole
salsas

MARINADE

¾ cup (180 ml/6 fl oz) fresh lime
juice
6 cloves garlic, crushed
2 tablespoons Worcestershire sauce
½ cup (80 ml/2½ fl oz) tequila
(optional)
3 tablespoons red wine
pinch dried oregano
pinch ground cumin
pinch sugar

33

1 To Make Marinade: combine lime juice, garlic, Worcestershire sauce, tequila, wine, oregano, cumin and sugar. Season to taste with freshly ground black pepper and salt. Place beef in a ceramic dish and pour over marinade. Cover with plastic wrap and set aside to marinate in the refrigerator for at least 1 hour, or overnight.

2 Heat oil in a heavy-based frypan and sear beef over a high heat for 3 to 4 minutes each side or until cooked to your liking, being careful not to overcook. (Alternatively, barbecue over a high heat.)

3 Slice meat thinly across the grain, sprinkle with coriander, and serve immediately either in the skillet in which it was cooked or on a warm serving plate. Allow people to help themselves to warm soft tortillas to wrap the meat in, and a choice of side dishes.

SERVES 4 TO 6

VARIATION: Chicken, veal, pork and even prawns can also be cooked in this way.

Madras Prawn Curry

INDIA

20 g (⅔ oz) ghee

1 onion, finely chopped

2 cloves garlic, crushed

1 tablespoon curry powder

250 g (8 oz) fresh tomatoes, peeled and chopped

2 tablespoons fresh lemon juice

500 g (16 oz) cooked prawns

1 Peel prawns leaving tails intact, remove back vein.

2 Melt ghee in a frying pan, sauté onion and garlic until onion is tender. Add curry powder, sauté 2 minutes.

3 Add tomatoes and lemon juice. Cover, bring to the boil, reduce heat to low, simmer for 10 minutes or until tomatoes are pulpy.

4 Add prawns, continue cooking until prawns are heated through.

SERVES 4

35

Pork Salad with Chili, Peanuts and Ginger
(Nam Sod) THAILAND

500 g (1 lb) fresh lean pork,
minced or finely chopped
2 tablespoons water
2 tablespoons lemon juice
2 tablespoons fish sauce
½ teaspoon dried chili
1 teaspoon finely sliced fresh chili
2 tablespoons finely sliced onion
2 tablespoons sliced shallots, cut into 2 cm (¾ in) pieces
2 tablespoons roasted peanuts
2 tablespoons finely sliced fresh ginger root
1 tablespoon fresh mint leaves
2 tablespoons chopped fresh coriander leaves and stems
6 large lettuce leaves

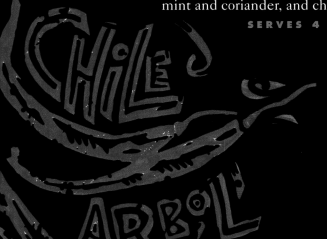

GARNISH

roasted peanuts, 1 tablespoon finely sliced ginger, dried and fresh chili, mint and coriander sprigs, and chili flowers (see page 38).

1 In a large saucepan place minced pork with 2 tablespoons water; cook slowly over medium heat until pork is cooked through but still tender.

2 Remove from heat and add lemon juice, fish sauce, dried and fresh chili. Stir and when cooled add onion, shallots, peanuts, ginger, mint and coriander leaves. Toss lightly.

3 Serve on a bed of lettuce leaves and garnish with mounds of peanuts, ginger and chili. Decorate with sprigs of mint and coriander, and chili flowers.

SERVES 4

CHILI FLOWER

1 Holding the stem with your finger, place chili on cutting board, then slit chili several times lengthways, cutting from the base to the point.

2 The cuts can be made spiky to give jagged edges.

3 Place into iced water and petals will curl out. Usually the more cuts and the finer they are, the more the petals will curl. Remove seeds after the flowers have opened.

Tandoori Chicken
INDIAN

8 chicken thighs, skin removed
1 large onion, chopped
4 cloves garlic, chopped
½ teaspoon ground ginger
1 teaspoon ground coriander
½ teaspoon ground cumin
2 teaspoons ground turmeric
½ teaspoon chili powder
½ cup (125 ml/4 fl oz) plain yoghurt
1 tablespoon white vinegar
1 tablespoon Worcestershire sauce
4 tablespoons fresh lemon juice
1 teaspoon garam masala

1 Make 3 or 4 cuts on each side of the chicken pieces.
2 Combine onion, garlic, ginger, coriander, cumin, turmeric, chili, yoghurt, vinegar, Worcestershire sauce and half the lemon juice in a blender or food processor. Blend until smooth.

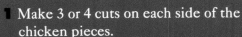

39

3 Pour spice mixture over chicken, refrigerate at least 6 hours, preferably overnight.

4 Place chicken on a rack in a baking dish. Bake in moderately hot oven for 45 minutes or until chicken is tender.

5 Sprinkle with garam masala and remaining lemon juice to serve.

SERVES 4 TO 6

Chili Con Carne
MEXICO

3 tablespoons vegetable oil
1 kg (2 lb) lean minced beef
1 medium onion, peeled and chopped
1 green capsicum (pepper), chopped
1 clove garlic, crushed
3 to 4 fresh birdseye chilies, finely chopped
1 to 2 teaspoons chili powder
1 teaspoon ground cumin
1 teaspoon paprika
½ teaspoon dried oregano
1 teaspoon sugar
1 bay leaf
440 g (14 oz) canned tomatoes,
undrained and mashed
440 g (14 oz) canned kidney or pinto beans
2 cups (500 ml/16 fl oz) beef stock
1 tablespoon plain flour, mixed to a
smooth paste with 3 tablespoons water
1 tablespoon cornmeal (polenta)

1 Heat oil in a large heavy-based saucepan and cook minced beef, onion, capsicum and garlic over a medium high heat until meat is browned. Add fresh chilies, chili powder, cumin, paprika, oregano, sugar, bay leaf, tomatoes, stock and beans and stir over heat for 2 minutes to combine. Reduce heat and simmer 1 hour, stirring occasionally.

2 Add flour mixture and cornmeal and cook, stirring constantly, until thickened. Serve with rice and tortillas and sour cream if desired.

SERVES 4

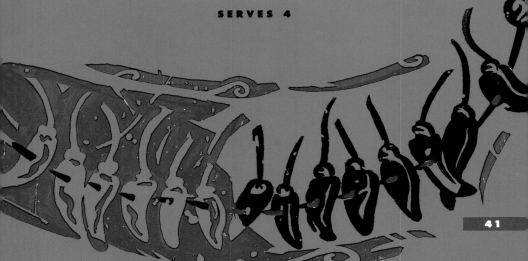

41

Spicy Chicken Livers
(Thab Gai Pad Prikon) T H A I L A N D

300 g (10 oz) chicken livers
6 dried Chinese mushrooms,
soaked for 20 minutes
in hot water
2 tablespoons vegetable oil
1 clove garlic,
finely chopped
2 medium-sized onions, sliced
2 fresh red chilies,
finely sliced
2 tablespoons fish sauce
1 teaspoon sugar
2 tablespoons lemon juice
½ green capsicum, sliced
3 shallots, cut in 3 cm pieces

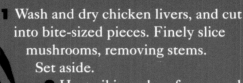

1 Wash and dry chicken livers, and cut into bite-sized pieces. Finely slice mushrooms, removing stems. Set aside.

2 Heat oil in wok or frypan and stir-fry garlic until golden, then add onions and chilies and stir-fry for 1 minute.

3 Add chicken livers, stir-fry until just pink, then add fish sauce, sugar, lemon juice and mushrooms. Stir-fry for another minute and check taste to see if more fish sauce, sugar or lemon juice is needed.

4 Stir in capsicum and shallots, stir-fry another minute and serve with rice.

SERVES 4

Prawns in Garlic and Chili Sauce
INDIA

1 kg (2 lb) uncooked king prawns
3 cloves garlic, crushed
2 teaspoons sugar
1 teaspoon soy sauce
½ teaspoon sesame oil
2 tablespoons cornflour
5 tablespoons oil
2 teaspoons oyster sauce
2 tablespoons water
1 tablespoon ginger wine
1 tablespoon chili sauce
1 tablespoon tomato sauce
1 large onion, chopped
1 green or red capsicum (pepper), chopped
2 spring onions, chopped

1 Peel prawns leaving tail intact, and remove back vein.

2 Combine prawns in a bowl with garlic, sugar, soy sauce, sesame oil and 1 tablespoon of the cornflour. Mix well, stand 10 minutes.

3 Heat 4 tablespoons of oil in a frying pan and fry prawns for 5 minutes. Remove.

4 Combine remaining 1 tablespoon cornflour with oyster sauce, water, ginger wine, chili sauce and tomato sauce.

5 Heat remaining 1 tablespoon oil in a saucepan, sauté onion and capsicum for 2 minutes.

6 Add prawns and cornflour mixture, stir over heat for 5 minutes or until sauce has thickened. Add spring onions.

SERVES 6 TO 8

Thai Barbecued Chicken
(Gai Yahng) THAILAND

1 kg (2 lb) chicken pieces, slightly larger than bite-sized (see *Note*)

MARINADE

1 tablespoon chopped coriander root and stem

1 tablespoon chopped garlic

1 teaspoon pepper

1 teaspoon sugar

1 teaspoon salt

2 teaspoons ground turmeric

3 tablespoons vegetable oil

1 Combine all marinade ingredients in a food processor or crush with a mortar and pestle.

2 Rub chicken pieces with marinade, and leave covered for at least 10 minutes, or preferably overnight, in the refrigerator.

3 Barbecue over hot coals or grill slowly until thoroughly cooked and slightly charred.

4 Serve with a spicy Thai sauce and rice.

NOTE: You can barbecue large chicken pieces and chop into smaller pieces with a mallet before serving, or split the larger limbs and slightly flatten them, so they cook easily.

SERVES 4

Seafood in Green Chili Sauce
(Pescado y Mariscos en Salsa Verde)
M E X I C O

100 g (3½ oz) white fish fillets, cut into
small pieces
1 small cooked crab, jointed
500 g (16 oz) raw prawns
10 mussels, cleaned and bearded
10 small clams or scallops

STOCK

6 cups (1½ litres/2½ pints) water
2 red snapper heads
2 cups fresh prawn heads (optional)
1 cup (250 ml/8 fl oz) dry white wine
4 carrots, peeled and quartered
1 leek, washed, cut lengthways and
quartered
1 onion, peeled and quartered
1 turnip, peeled and quartered (optional)

14 cloves garlic
small bunch fresh parsley,
chopped
2 bay leaves
1 teaspoon black peppercorns

GREEN CHILI SAUCE

6 poblano chilies (if
unavailable substitute 4 fresh
large hot green chilies and 2
medium green capsicums
(peppers), seeded and
chopped
1 large onion, peeled and
chopped
small bunch fresh parsley,
chopped
small bunch fresh coriander,
chopped
4 cloves garlic
⅓ cup (80 ml/2½ fl oz)
chili sauce

1 To Make Stock: Place water, fish and prawn heads, wine, carrots, leeks, onion, turnip, garlic, parsley, bay leaves and pepper in a large saucepan or stock pot and simmer, uncovered, over a low heat for 1 hour. Strain into a bowl, reserving vegetables and discarding heads. Set aside and allow to cool.

2 Place ¾ cup (180 ml/6 fl oz) cooled stock and vegetables in a food processor or blender and process until smooth. Return purée to remaining strained stock, stir and set aside.

3 To Make Sauce: Place chilies, onion, parsley, coriander, garlic and 1 cup (250 ml/8 fl oz) cooled fish stock mixture in a food processor and blend until well combined.

4 Place blended ingredients and chili sauce in a large heavy-based saucepan and cook over a medium heat for 2 to 3 minutes to release flavors. Add 2 cups (500 ml/16 fl oz) remaining fish stock and simmer for 15 to 20 minutes or until sauce reaches desired consistency. (If desired you can add more blended parsley or coriander, chilies, or chili sauce to strengthen the flavor.)

5 Add assorted seafood, cover and cook on medium heat for 4 to 6 minutes or until mussels open and prawns change color. Season to taste with freshly ground black pepper and salt.

SERVES 6

SEAFOOD IN GREEN CHILI SAUCE

This stunning seafood dish makes a
wonderful centrepiece for a Mexican fiesta,
or can be served as a meal in itself with
fresh crusty bread or freshly warmed
tortillas. You can make this dish
two ways — as a Mexican style
bouillabaisse served in soup
bowls, or using less stock,
reducing to a thick sauce,
and serving it as a seafood
casserole with rice.

Salmon with Coconut Coriander Salsa

6 salmon cutlets
60 g (2 oz) butter
3 tablespoons fresh lemon juice

SALSA

1 cup (90 g/3 oz) desiccated coconut
3 tablespoons water
2 green chilies, seeded and chopped
2 teaspoons oil
1 teaspoon black mustard seeds
3 tablespoons chopped fresh coriander

1 Wash and dry salmon. Place butter and lemon juice on a hot barbecue plate and heat until foaming. Cook salmon until tender.

2 To Make Salsa: Place coconut, water and chili in a food processor or blender and process until smooth. Heat oil in a small pan, add mustard seeds and cook until they pop.

3 Add coconut mixture and cook for a further 3 minutes. Stir through coriander. Serve salmon with warm or cold salsa.

SERVES 6

Chili Pepper Yabbies

12 uncooked yabbies or scampi

MARINADE

2 red chilies, seeded and chopped

½ cup (125 ml/4 fl oz) tomato purée

2 cloves garlic, crushed

6 spring onions, thinly sliced

2 tablespoons chopped fresh basil

3 teaspoons cracked black pepper

1 Make a small slit on the underside of each tail to allow marinade to soak through.

2 To Make Marinade: Place chili, tomato purée, garlic, onions, basil and pepper in a large bowl and mix to combine. Add yabbies, cover and refrigerate for 1 hour.

3 Cook yabbies on a hot barbeque plate with marinade for 10 to 15 minutes or until flesh is tender. Serve with a leafy salad, and provide guests with nutcrackers.

SERVES 6

Red Chili Salsa
(Salsa Roja) M E X I C O

170 g (6 oz) fresh hot red chilies, seeded
3 cups (750 ml/24 fl oz) hot water
3 tablespoons tomato paste
1 garlic clove, crushed
3 tablespoons olive oil
pinch salt
¼ teaspoon ground cumin
1 teaspoon finely chopped fresh oregano
1 teaspoon finely chopped fresh coriander

1 Rinse chilies in cool water. Place in a bowl, cover with hot water and allow to soak for 1 hour. (Alternately steam them for 5 minutes.)
2 Place chilies and remaining ingredients in a food processor or blender with a little extra water and process until coarsely chopped.
3 Place mixture in a saucepan and simmer slowly for 10 minutes, stirring occasionally, or until sauce reaches the desired consistency.

MAKES 3 ½ CUPS (875 ML/36 FL OZ)

Hot Peach Pickle
INDIA

1 kg (2 lb) nearly ripe peaches
3 cups (500 g/16 oz)
brown sugar
1½ cups (375 ml/12 fl oz)
white vinegar
250 g (8 oz) seedless sultanas
30 g (1 oz) red chilies,
sliced and seeds removed
1 teaspoon ground ginger

1 Blanch peaches in very hot water for 1 minute, remove, peel off skins. Cut peaches in half, remove seeds.

2 Combine sugar and half the vinegar in a saucepan, bring to the boil.

3 Add peaches, reduce heat to low. Cover and simmer until peaches are soft.

4 Add sultanas, chilies, ginger and remaining vinegar. Simmer, uncovered, until mixture has reduced and thickened.

5 When cool, pour into sterilised jars, seal well.

MAKES 4 CUPS
(1 LITRE/35 FL OZ)

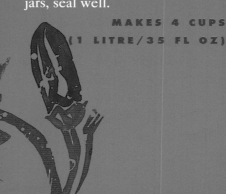

Eggplant Pickle
INDIA

2 kg (4½ lb) eggplant (aubergine),
cut into 2.5 cm (1 in) pieces
125 g (4 oz) green chilies, chopped
2 cloves garlic, crushed
1½ cups (625 ml/21 fl oz)
white vinegar
2 tablespoons chili powder
2 teaspoons ground turmeric
2 teaspoons ground ginger
1¼ cups (310 ml/10 fl oz)
sesame oil
1 tablespoon cumin seeds
1 tablespoon fenugreek seeds
2 heaped tablespoons salt
1 cup (250 g/8 oz) sugar
30 g (1 oz) fresh ginger,
finely chopped

1 Combine garlic with
1 tablespoon vinegar, chili
powder, turmeric and ground
ginger, to form a paste.

2 Heat oil to moderate, fry cumin
and fenugreek seeds for
1 minute.

3 Add the spice paste, stir over
low heat until oil floats on top.

4 Add remaining vinegar, salt,
sugar, eggplant, chilies and
fresh ginger. Stir over low heat
until oil floats on top again.

5 When cool, pour into sterilised
jars, seal well.

**MAKES 5 CUPS
(1 ¼ LITRES/2 PINTS)**

Pickled Chilies

(Chiles Encurtidos) M E X I C O

Jalapeño or serrano chilies are
ideal for this dish.

6 cups (1½ litres/2½ pints) water
1 cup (250 ml/8 fl oz) vinegar
½ cup (125 ml/4 fl oz) vegetable oil
5 bay leaves
2 tablespoons chopped fresh
marjoram or ½ teaspoon
dried marjoram
2 tablespoons chopped fresh thyme or
½ teaspoon dried thyme
1 tablespoon dried oregano
1 tablespoon cracked black pepper
2 onions, peeled and quartered
20 cloves garlic, peeled
½ kg (1 lb) fresh small red chilies

1 Combine water, vinegar, oil,
herbs, pepper, onion, and
garlic in a large heavy-
based saucepan. Bring to
the boil and add chilies.
Boil rapidly for 2 minutes,
then cover pot and remove
from heat. Allow to stand
overnight.

2 Spoon chilies into hot
sterilised jars, cover with
cooking liquid and seal.
Store in a cool, dark place.

MAKES ABOUT FIVE 1 CUP
(250 ML/8 FL OZ) JARS

Hot Pickled Vegetables
(Pak Dong) THAILAND

3 cups (750 ml/24 fl oz) white vinegar

1½ tablespoons sugar

2 teaspoons salt

250 g (8 oz) cauliflower pieces

250 g (8 oz) cucumber, peeled,
seeded and diced

250 g (8 oz) baby corn

100 g (3½ oz) broccoli, bok choy
or Chinese broccoli pieces

200 g (6½ oz) cabbage, cut into pieces

4 cloves garlic, finely chopped

1 medium-sized onion, finely chopped

6 dried red chilies, seeded and chopped

1 cup (250 ml/8 fl oz) peanut oil

1 tablespoon sesame seeds, dry-fried to golden, and fresh coriander
leaves, to garnish

1 In a large saucepan, bring vinegar, sugar and salt to the boil. Add all the vegetables (except garlic, onion and chilies) and blanch for about 1 minute, ensuring they remain crisp. (The leafy vegetables will probably need less cooking time, so use your discretion). Remove from heat and put aside, leaving vegetables to stand in the vinegar syrup.

2 In a food processor, combine the garlic, onion and chilies and blend to a smooth paste.

3 In a wok or large frypan, heat oil and stir-fry paste for several minutes, then add blanched vegetables and their syrup. Stir and cook for about 1 minute, combining flavors but being careful not to break up the vegetables or overcook them.

4 Serve warm on a dish sprinkled with roasted sesame seeds and garnish with coriander, or cool and pour into sterilised jars for later use. If covered tightly, jars can be stored for a week or two.

SERVES 4

Bengal Apple Chutney
INDIA

8 large cooking apples
1½ cups (250 g/8 oz) brown sugar
3½ cups (900 ml/1½ pints) malt vinegar
30 g (1 oz) fresh ginger, grated
½ onion, finely chopped
3 cloves garlic, crushed
1½ tablespoons mustard seeds
2 teaspoons salt
2 to 3 teaspoons chili powder
¾ cup (125 g/4 oz) raisins

1 Peel and slice apples, combine, in a saucepan, with sugar and vinegar, bring to boil. Cover, reduce heat to low, simmer until apples are tender.

2 Add ginger, onion, garlic, mustard seeds, salt, chili powder and raisins. Simmer, uncovered, for 15 minutes or until mixture has reduced and thickened, stirring often.

3 When cool, seal in sterilised jars.

MAKES 6 CUPS (1½ LITRES/2½ PINTS)

Stuffed Chilies
(Chiles Rellenos) M E X I C O

8 canned or fresh poblano chilies or 8 fresh
banana or other large chilies
(12 to 15 cm [4½ to 6 in] in length)
½ cup (60 g/2 oz) plain flour
3 eggs, separated
1 teaspoon salt
vegetable oil for cooking
2 tablespoons chopped fresh coriander
chili sauce of your choice

MEAT FILLING

1 tablespoon vegetable oil
2 tablespoons finely chopped onion
1 clove garlic, crushed
250 g (8 oz) minced beef
2 tomatoes, peeled, seeded and chopped
1 small bay leaf
5 almonds, chopped
1 tablespoon raisins

59

1 Drain canned chilies, rinse and make a slit vertically down the side of each. Remove the seeds and pith. Prepare fresh chilies by placing under a preheated hot grill and cook until the skin chars and blisters. Place in a sealed plastic bag for 10 minutes to sweat off skin. Remove skin film by raking over the surface of chili with a spoon. Slit open and remove the seeds and veins, retaining the stems. If using banana chilies, rub the insides with chili powder.

2 To Make Filling: Heat oil in a frypan and cook onion and garlic over a medium heat until onions are soft. Add beef and cook until browned. Add tomatoes and bay leaf, reduce heat and simmer for 15 minutes. Season to taste. Mix in almonds and raisins and remove from heat. Set aside and allow to cool. Fill each chili with 2 tablespoons of the filling, being careful not to overfill them. Overlap the edges to enclose the filling.

3 Roll each chili in flour, coating lightly.

4 Heat enough oil in a large frypan to cover 2 cm (¾ in) deep.

5 Beat the egg whites with salt until soft peaks form. In a separate bowl, beat egg yolks until thick and creamy. Fold gently into the egg whites. Dip floured chilies into egg batter and cook in oil over a medium high heat, for 4 to 5 minutes each side until cooked through. Remove and drain on absorbent paper.

6 Serve immediately, sprinkled with coriander and chili sauce.

SERVES 4

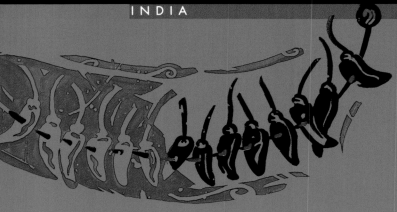

Egg Sambal

4 hard-boiled eggs, halved
lengthways
½ small onion, finely chopped
1 green chili, finely chopped
1 tablespoon oil
1 tablespoon lemon juice
2 tablespoons desiccated coconut

1 Combine eggs, onion, chili, oil and lemon juice.

2 Sprinkle with desiccated or fresh grated coconut, just before serving.

SERVES 4

Mixed Vegetable Sambal

2 carrots, finely diced
½ cup shelled peas
60 g (2 oz) green beans, cut into
   1 cm (¼ in) lengths
1 turnip, finely diced
1 potato, finely diced
2 green chilies, finely chopped
2 tablespoons lemon juice
2 tablespoons oil
desiccated coconut

1 Cook vegetables in boiling water until tender, drain.

2 Add chilies, lemon juice and oil, stir until combined.

3 Serve sprinkled with desiccated coconut.

SERVES 4

Potato Sambal

2 potatoes, cut into 1 cm (¼ in) cubes
1 green chili, finely chopped
1 pinch chili powder
2 spring onions, chopped
1 tablespoon oil
2 tablespoons lemon juice

1 Cook potatoes in boiling
water until tender, drain.
2 Combine potatoes with
remaining ingredients.

SERVES 4

AN ANGUS & ROBERTSON PUBLICATION

Angus&Robertson, an imprint of
HarperCollins*Publishers*

25 Ryde Road, Pymble, Sydney NSW 2073, Australia
31 View Road, Glenfield, Auckland 10, New Zealand
77–85 Fulham Palace Road, London W6 8JB, United Kingdom
10 East 53rd Street, New York NY 10022, USA

First published in Australia in 1994
Recipes pp 18, 20, 22, 23, 33, 40, 47, 52, 55 & 59 © Sharon Barkhurst
and Patricia Lake 1994
Recipes pp 14, 28, 32, 36, 42, 46 & 56 © Patricia Lake
and Somi Miller 1994

National Library of Australia
Cataloguing-in-Publication data:
Allardice, Pamela, 1958-.
Hot
ISBN 0 207 18596 4.
1. Cookery (Hot peppers). I. Title.
641. 6384

Design by Liz Seymour
Illustrations by Steven Bray
Printed in Hong Kong

9 8 7 6 5 4 3 2 1
98 97 96 95 94